The Hidden Majority

The Only Mathematically Feasible Solution to America's Broken Political System

by

Dale A. Berryhill
& Kevin P. Henry

DAB BOOKS

Copyright © 2025 by Dale A. Berryhill

All rights reserved. No part of this document may be reproduced in any manner whatsoever except in the case of brief quotations in critical articles and reviews.

Print ISBN 978-0-9883596-2-8
eBook ISBN 978-0-9883596-3-5

First Edition

DAB BOOKS

Published through IngramSpark
www.IngramSpark.com

Table of Contents

SUMMARY	1
PART ONE: THE OPPORTUNITY	3
• The Gap in the Middle	5
• Are There Really Enough Votes to Bring About Meaningful Change?	7
• The Hidden Majority	9
• How Do You Hide a Majority?	10
• How *Should* the Polls Be Read?	12
PART TWO: THE PROBLEM	13
• The Goal of the Major Parties	15
• Governing by Ideology	16
• What Do the American People Really Want?	17
• Why the Hidden Majority Can Govern Best	19
PART THREE: THE SOLUTION	21
• A New Agenda	23
• A New Alliance	24
• Do You Belong in the Hidden Majority Alliance?	25
• Does This Mean Compromising Your Values?	26
• What Are Our Options?	27
PART FOUR: THE LOGISTICS	29
• Should We Start with a New Third Party?	31
• The First Step	32
• Moving Forward	33
• Deciding Our Positions	34
• Hitting the Pause Button	35
PART FIVE: THE FAQs	37

Summary

Americans disagree on a lot of things, but they agree on one thing: Our political system is broken. So broken that it threatens the future stability of our nation.

The majority of Americans are unhappy with all three branches of our government. They are unhappy with both major parties. They are unhappy with the way things are going *even when their own party is in power*.

If this dissatisfied majority could be united and organized, it could affect elections, put pressure on the entrenched interests, and turn the focus of our government back to serving the American people.

Unfortunately, this majority is hidden by a nearly universal misreading of the polls. When that misreading is corrected, the Hidden Majority is revealed. And by looking at the Hidden Majority as a distinct target market, we can easily craft a mathematically feasible strategic plan for organizing America's unaffiliated and dissatisfied voters into an effective political force.

Of course, there have already been attempts to fix America's broken political system: third parties, independent candidates, reach-across-the-aisle efforts, election reform, and more. But none of these have slowed, much less stopped, our nation's partisan political polarization. Nor can they without recognizing and appealing to the Hidden Majority.

PART ONE
THE OPPORTUNITY

Politics is a numbers game. You can't win if you don't have the votes. And if you split the vote, you only make things worse.

Given America's tradition of a two-party system, and with the two major parties holding an iron grip on our government, surely any talk of real change is futile.

Or is it?

The Gap in the Middle

Let's say the bar graph below represents the American political spectrum, the left wing on the left and the right wing on the right. The line in the middle is the 50% mark each party must cross to get elected:

The major parties and the news media want you to believe that the American people are divided in a bipolar manner, Republican vs. Democrat, liberal vs. conservative, pro-life vs. pro-choice, with few voters in-between:

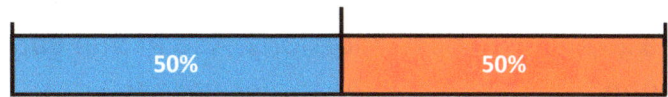

If that were true, there would be nothing anyone could do. If that were true, we would be doomed to never-ending gridlock and ever-increasing polarization.

But it's not true. In fact, it's a huge lie. Here's where Americans really stand:

1) PARTY AFFILIATION

According to Gallup*, fewer than 30% of Americans identify themselves with each of the two major parties:

2) IDEOLOGY

Gallup got similar results when asking people about their ideology. Those who call themselves "liberal" are on the left below, while those who call themselves "conservative" are on the right:

www.HiddenMajority.org

3) INDIVIDUAL ISSUES

It even holds true with individual issues. Two years after *Roe v. Wade* was overturned, 35% said abortion should be legal in all circumstances and 12% said it should be prohibited under all circumstances. Fifty-three percent—the majority of Americans—did not agree with either of these views:

This is the dirty little secret of our political system today: The major parties are divided in a bipolar manner, but the American people are not.

Whether we're talking about party affiliation, ideology, or specific issues, there is a gap in the middle—a gap of historic proportions. And in that gap is a group of voters *bigger than those supporting either of the major parties*.

In business parlance, this is called a "market opportunity."

In politics, it can mean a revolution.

*All polls are Gallup unless otherwise stated.

Are There Really Enough Votes to Bring About Meaningful Change?

Yes, there are. The dissatisfaction of the American voter goes deeper than you're being told:

1) UNAFFILIATED VOTERS

While the major parties each enjoy less than 30% support, more than four out of ten do not consider themselves affiliated with either:

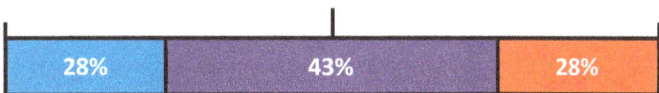

Which makes unaffiliated voters the largest voting bloc in America—by far. If they all voted the same way, they would win in a three-way election.

But that's just the beginning.

2) VOTERS WHO WANT A NEW THIRD PARTY

Since 2013, around 60% of Americans have said they want a new third party, one that can actually compete with the existing parties:

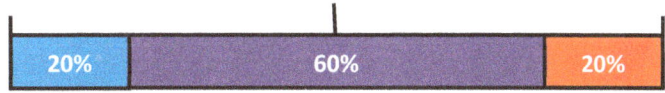

If these voters were united, they would win even in a two-way race—every time.

3) VOTERS UNHAPPY WITH OUR NATION'S DIRECTION

Since 2006, regardless of which party is in power, an average of around 70% have said America is headed in the wrong direction:

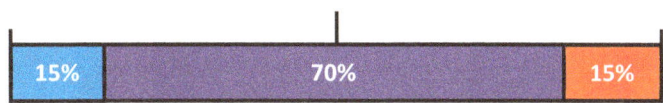

And we're still not through.

www.HiddenMajority.org

4) VOTERS UNHAPPY WITH OUR GOVERNMENT

Every president since George W. Bush has had less than 50% public approval for half or more of their time in office. In 2024, confidence in America's judicial system hit a record low of 26%. And since 2006, public approval of Congress has averaged around 20%:

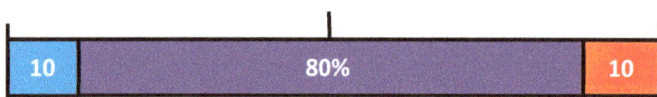

As you can see, America's dissatisfaction isn't confined to unaffiliated and independent voters. It goes deep into the ranks of Republicans and Democrats.

The fact is, the major parties do not have the support of most Americans, and the government they run does not have our trust. Yet they make all our laws, appoint all our judges, and issue all the regulations under which we live.

Given that fact, can we really claim to have a representative government in America today?

The Hidden Majority

As we've already shown you, 43% of voters do not identify themselves as being affiliated with either major party:

Which means that at least 72% do not agree with the Democratic party's agenda:

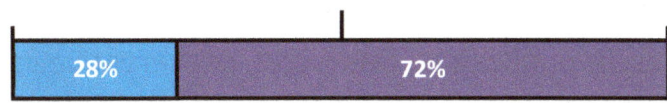

And at least 72% do not agree with the Republican party's agenda:

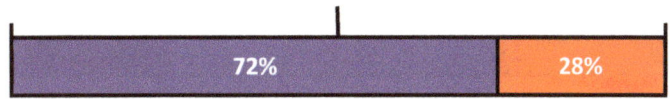

In other words, the only true majority in American politics today is the one that doesn't want *either* major party to have its way. That could explain why voters repeatedly balance the parties against each other so that neither can enact its full agenda.

Likewise, since 65% of Americans do not want abortion to be legal in every case and more than 85% don't want it to be illegal in every case, the only majority is the one that doesn't fully agree with the hardline positions on either end. The same is true with issues like gun control and immigration.

Yet despite being the majority, these groups are never heard from, in the media or in politics.

They are a majority without representation; they are a majority without a voice.

They are a Hidden Majority.

How Do You Hide a Majority?

Turns out it's pretty easy. Just focus everyone's attention on the most controversial issues, then allow only hardline voices in the media. Deride those willing to compromise as the "mushy middle." Dismiss the growing dissatisfaction of voters as an anti-establishment "mood" rather than a reasoned response to real failures in our government. Then justify it all with a misreading of the polls that reinforces the status quo and excludes dissenting voices.

Here's how it happens:

In keeping with our two-party system, polling firms usually begin by giving people two opposing choices, Republican vs. Democrat, conservative vs. liberal, pro-choice vs. pro-life. As we've already shown you, this is what Gallup got when asking about party affiliation:

For the respondents who don't choose one or the other, pollsters ask which way they "lean." Here's what Gallup got after asking this follow-up question:

Which is fine, except that these findings are invariably reported and discussed by politicians and the news media this way:

Voters who are more moderate—or whose views are more complex than the prechosen positions of the political establishment—get lumped in with the hardliners *even though they specifically declined to identify themselves that way*.

This may be why one in ten refuse to say they even lean one way or the other. Those one in ten are then discarded as "undecideds," when they are actually part of the Hidden Majority, the largest voting bloc in America today.

To see the result of this misreading, just compare the last bar graph above to those on the previous page. The 43% who disagree with both parties completely disappears. The 72% who disagree with each party completely disappears. The majority is completely hidden.

Which means that our entire public discourse is framed around a skewed view of what the American people want.

How *Should* the Polls be Read?

Asking follow-up questions of middle-ground voters—then using their answers to lump them in with hardliners—might have made sense when they were fewer in number. It makes no sense now that they are the largest voting bloc in America.

As it is, we're doing it backwards. We're using the polls to evaluate how closely the American people align with the agendas of the major parties when we should be evaluating how well the parties and politicians reflect the will of the people.

So, how *should* the polls be read?

Simply put, those who do not align with the establishment parties or positions are a separate group and should be treated as such. This is, after all, the category they placed themselves in when asked. They are not "undecided," and they are not "leaners"—they are independent-minded people who reject the hardline positions of the major parties. And they are the majority.

When we look at the Hidden Majority as a distinct group, we see that there is already a contingency for a third option in American politics. The votes are already there. The only reason this majority isn't viewed as a separate group is that it isn't organized and has no party to vote for on election day.

So why don't we have a viable third party, or at least an organized movement? Because no one has put together a plan addressing the needs of the dissatisfied voters who make up the largest voting bloc in America today. No one has put together a plan targeting the Hidden Majority.

Until now.

PART TWO
THE PROBLEM

Support for real change in America's political system is more than strong enough to put pressure on the powers-that-be, but only if the Hidden Majority is united. To find out how that might happen, let's make sure we understand exactly what divides us in the first place.

The Goal of the Major Parties

If we were to ask you to describe today's Democrat or Republican parties, you would no doubt begin listing their ideological positions:

- Republicans are the party of the Right; Democrats are the party of the Left.
- Democrats are pro-choice and pro-gay rights; Republicans are not.
- Republicans are pro-gun rights and pro-death penalty; Democrats are not.
- Democrats accuse Republicans of favoring the rich; Republicans accuse Democrats of communistic schemes to redistribute wealth.

The major parties are defined—by themselves and by each other—by their stances on controversial ideological issues.

Now, what if we were to ask you which party is known for being honest and transparent? Or for being responsible trustees of our tax dollars? Or for delivering government services effectively and efficiently?

What if we asked you which party is known for rejecting the influence of the special interests? Or for refusing to manipulate the rules in order to pass or block legislation? Or for making decisions wisely, in an organized, rational manner?

On the state and local level, you could probably tell us which party wants an open carry law for guns or a non-discrimination ordinance for transgender individuals. But can you tell us which party is known for keeping the potholes filled and the lines at the DMV short? Can you tell us which party is successfully educating your children while protecting you and your family from theft and violence?

You see, the Republicans and the Democrats aren't trying to prove which of them can do a better job of running the country. They're not competing to see who can be the most professional, the most honest, or the most responsive to the wishes of the people they represent. What they are fighting for is control of our government so they can use it to impose their ideological agendas on us, with or without our consent.

They are proving this by sticking to those agendas even as they lose market share.

Governing by Ideology

With the notable exception of slavery, political differences in the first half of American history focused on how the government should be run. Today, they focus on how government should run society.

Governing by ideology means using governmental authority to bring about your vision of how you think the world should be. That might be fine if we all agreed on the same vision, but clearly we don't.

Despite this, both major parties are engaged in ongoing efforts to pass laws and secure court decisions that are not supported by the majority of Americans. They do this regularly, knowingly, and blatantly, and they've been doing it for so long that we've stopped noticing how inappropriate it is. We've stopped noticing that it is the very antithesis of what a representative government is supposed to be.

How *should* these issues be decided? In a free society with a representative government, controversial social issues should be decided by the people, in the marketplace of ideas. Those who want to change our society and culture (including changing them back) should focus on changing the hearts and minds of the American people, not on filing lawsuits and lobbying politicians. If they succeed in persuading people to their way of thinking, a representative government will naturally follow.

That's certainly not what the major parties are doing today. Instead, they are relying increasingly on executive orders and judicial mandates, jettisoning longstanding legislative traditions, fiddling with how elections are held, and urging their members to take to the street. Both major parties are abandoning the democratic process precisely because they can't get a majority of Americans to support their hardline agendas.

And what has been the result? Legislative gridlock and runaway deficits. Riots and social unrest. The politicization of our judicial system. "Slippery slope" arguments in which commonsense reforms favored by the majority are rejected for fear they will lead to a complete loss of freedoms.

The more ideological the major parties have become, the more they have sown disunity and ignored the basic functions of government. And the more they have lost the support of the American people.

What Do the American People Really Want?

While the ideological hardliners dominate the conversation, the polls show that the vast majority of Americans are reasonable, even charitable people who want commonsense, middle-ground approaches to our social problems. This holds true for even the most controversial issues:

Reproductive Rights

While six out of ten Americans did not agree with overturning *Roe v. Wade*, only 37% believe abortion should be legal after the first trimester and 22% after the second trimester. Despite what the two sides claim, there is no consensus for making abortion either legal or illegal in all cases. However, there is a consensus for treating it like other medical procedures: 87% of Americans favor full disclosure of the medical risks prior to an abortion, 71% favor parental approval for girls under 18, and 69% favor a 24-hour waiting period.

Gun Rights

Most Americans favor individual gun rights, but according to a 2023 Fox News poll, around 80% favor red flag laws, universal background checks, and a waiting period for gun purchases. Gallup found that while 56% of Americans favor stricter gun laws, only 20% support a ban on handguns, by far the weapon most used in gun crimes. More people favor increased funding for mental health care than support gun bans.

Economics

A distinct majority of Americans oppose calls for more economic government control in the form of socialism. In addition, both Gallup and Pew Research have found that people define socialism in so many different ways that accurate polling is difficult, if not impossible. On the other end of the spectrum, the libertarian idea of unfettered capitalism (including calls for the elimination of antidiscrimination laws in hiring and even in serving customers) also lacks support. Polls consistently find around one in ten identifying as libertarian, but Pew Research points out that only half of those actually know what it means. Rejecting both of these hardline ideological positions, the American people overwhelmingly desire a free-market system with reasonable government oversight.

Immigration

While 53% of Americans favor building a wall along the southern border, 70% favor a pathway to citizenship for illegals already in the country. Similarly, while 77% feel the situation at the U.S.-Mexico border is a major problem or even a crisis, 64% say they are sympathetic toward illegal immigrants. Sixty-four percent say immigration is a good thing overall, but 86% think that large numbers of immigrants entering the country illegally is a serious threat to our nation.

Racial Discrimination

A 2023 study by Public Agenda found that 91% of Americans believe in equal opportunity for all races, and 63% feel that race still impacts that opportunity. However, that same poll found that 77% believe people are too quick to raise charges of racism, with 68% of black Americans agreeing. Pew Research found that 52% believe the U.S. has made great strides over the past sixty years, but the same percentage feels we haven't done enough. Meanwhile, after "Defund the Police" became a rallying cry for protestors in 2020, Gallup found that 81% of black Americans want the police presence in their neighborhood to stay the same or increase.

Do these figures match what you see on television every night? Do they match what the two sides are saying about each other? Or is the truth being hidden along with the majority?

What we're actually seeing in these polls is the American people striving for fair and reasonable approaches to our social problems. They are not compromising their values; these *are* their values. And they are the majority.

Which leads us to an astonishing truth: These issues aren't really controversial! They only *appear* controversial because the majority has been chopped up and reassigned to the hardliners at each end. In reality, the majority of Americans agree on how these problems should be handled, and they have all along.

If our government truly represented the positions of the people instead of the ideological agendas of the major parties, these so-called "hot button" issues would not be dividing our nation.

Why the Hidden Majority Can Govern Best

We've all been conditioned by the media and the politicians to focus on arguments over individual issues. But there can also be differences in the way people approach political issues in general. And that is where we find a fundamental distinction between the Hidden Majority and the ideological hardliners.

While the hardliners at each end of the spectrum despise each other, they're actually identical in their approach to social and political issues. Both sides are absolutists who see everything in terms of black and white, with no gray areas. No exceptions and no compromises are allowed, so negotiation is impossible. In fact, they don't *want* to negotiate; they want to win the battle and impose their visions on the rest of us.

Members of the Hidden Majority, on the other hand, recognize the complexities of life and of politics. They understand that not every societal problem can be permanently cured and that sometimes the best we can do is try to balance conflicting interests. Whether they lean left or right, they could negotiate and implement reasonable solutions. They could do this because they are not attempting to impose their views on the nation.

Can the Hidden Majority be united? The Hidden Majority is *already* united by their more reasonable approach to social and political issues.

Now we see why the entrenched interests work so hard to keep the Hidden Majority hidden: They don't want us to notice that the real disagreement in America today isn't between liberals and conservatives. *The real disagreement in America today is between the dogmatic hardliners and the pragmatic majority.*

Unfortunately, there is no organized movement representing those who favor a more balanced approach to government.

Perhaps it's time to start one.

PART THREE
THE SOLUTION

The Hidden Majority represents a paradigm-shifting opportunity in American politics. But this opportunity can only be realized through an agenda that addresses the unmet needs of this specific target audience. In order to succeed, the movement must be built around the values of the American people, not the opinions of the organizers.

Luckily, this is easily accomplished by simply refocusing on the core responsibilities of government.

A New Agenda

The alternative to governing by ideology is to focus on practical matters first. To prove you can handle the basic responsibilities of government before you try to save the world. To return to the idea of running the government instead of running society.

Most importantly, it means returning to a government that truly represents the people.

What if there were a party or movement:

- whose only agenda was the delivery of government services in a professional, consumer-oriented fashion?
- whose only goal was to operate our government effectively, efficiently, and transparently?
- that didn't push or support a specific ideological agenda, but instead allowed disagreements to be resolved through the marketplace of ideas?
- that stopped catering to the hardliners on each end and instead sought to represent the broad middle ground of the American people?

A government run by such a party wouldn't bounce back and forth between the policies of opposing factions after every election. It wouldn't spend all its time and energy attacking and investigating the other side. Instead, it would focus on serving the needs of the people. In doing so, it would restore stability to our government.

Our two-party system has worked so well for so long because the major parties stayed in the mainstream, leaving the radicals on the fringes. But today the radicals are at home in the major parties, and it is the middle-ground American who is left without a party and without a voice.

A party or movement with a citizen-oriented agenda could capture the votes that the major parties can no longer take for granted.

A New Alliance

Today's political alliances are based on race, class, gender, religion, sexual orientation, and, most importantly, ideology. These alliances divide Americans rather than uniting them. And as long as Americans remain divided against each other, the major parties and the special interests will continue to run roughshod over the people.

There is one place where the American people are not divided, and that is in their belief that our government is failing us. So why not unite to change the government? Why not form an alliance of those who want our government to serve the people instead of pushing agendas? Why not form an alliance of the Hidden Majority?

A party or movement with a citizen-oriented agenda would automatically appeal to a new alliance. It would be an alliance of those who:

- want balanced, commonsense approaches to our social problems.
- demand truth and transparency from the government even when it makes their own party look bad.
- don't want their party playing parliamentary tricks to pass or block legislation.
- believe public policy issues should be decided calmly and rationally, not by shouting, not by name-calling, and not by intimidation.

The members of this new alliance don't have to agree on everything. In fact, they only have to agree on one thing:

Our government's agenda should come from the people, not from the parties, not from the media, and not from the special interests.

Do You Belong in the Hidden Majority Alliance?

A Hidden Majority Alliance would have nothing to do with whether you're black or white, male or female, young or old.

It would have nothing to do with whether you're rich or poor, gay or straight, religious or atheist.

It wouldn't even matter whether you're liberal or conservative. You could be a registered Democrat or Republican and still be part of the Hidden Majority.

- If you agree that our government is failing to fulfill its basic responsibilities, you are part of the Hidden Majority Alliance.

- If you feel government should serve the American people instead of controlling them and spying on them, you're part of the Hidden Majority Alliance.

- If you're tired of the partisan bickering and government shutdowns, you're part of the Hidden Majority Alliance.

- If you're concerned about how your taxes are being spent and worry that the other side might take away your rights, you're part of the Hidden Majority Alliance.

- If you don't agree with the more radical goals of either side, you are part of the Hidden Majority Alliance.

To be a part of the Hidden Majority Alliance, you only have to be the type of person who recognizes the complexities of life and understands the need to balance competing needs and interests. The type of person who respects opposing viewpoints. The type who abides by the democratic process even when it doesn't deliver what you want when you want it.

It's as simple as that.

Does This Mean Compromising Your Values?

An alliance based on the views of the Hidden Majority would not require anyone to compromise their values. Here's why:

First, a new party or movement doesn't require anyone to do anything. Everyone is still free to vote for whomever they choose. This would just be a new option for those who want it.

Second, this approach is not an attempt to sway people to our way of thinking. Rather, it's an attempt to provide representation for an existing group whose values are currently being ignored.

Third, voting for Hidden Majority candidates doesn't mean you can't continue to fight for whatever cause you choose. We're not trying to suppress controversial ideological debates; we just want to move them out of the halls of government and back into the marketplace of ideas, where they belong.

Fourth, joining the Hidden Majority Alliance doesn't mean you have to change your beliefs in any way. It just means you recognize that our nation needs a more balanced approach.

After all, what's the point of fighting over specific issues when the entire system is dissolving into chaos?

What Are Our Options?

In this document, we have demonstrated just how far the major parties and their allies have strayed from the views of the people they supposedly represent. What are our options for repairing this dichotomy?

1) Well, we could do nothing.
Currently, our political system is captive to two warring factions creating widening rifts in our society. If we continue as we are, either the whole system will fall apart, or one of these two sides will win the battle. But since neither side represents anything even approaching a majority, winning the battle could only occur by throwing out the rules and using force or the threat of force. Unfortunately, we are already seeing people on both sides willing to do just that.

2) We could try to reform the major parties.
Sadly, the major parties show no openness to the idea of reining themselves in. On the contrary, they seem to be increasingly controlled by their more radical wings. They are unlikely to reconsider their trend toward extremism unless they start getting pressure from, and even losing votes to, a less hardline option. In that sense, giving voice to the Hidden Majority *is* the way to reform the major parties.

3) We can keep trying to find a solution without the Hidden Majority.
As mentioned in our opening statement, there have already been efforts to fix our system—third parties, independent candidates, reach-across-the-aisle programs, election reform, and more. None of these attempts have recognized the Hidden Majority or tried to appeal to it specifically. As a result, none of them have the voter base necessary to put even a dent in our growing partisanship. But many of these efforts *could* be productive if they were based on the views and desires of the Hidden Majority. Which brings us to our best bet:

4) We could organize and give voice to the Hidden Majority.
When you think about it, it's truly amazing that the largest voting bloc in America has no spokesperson, no organization, and no political machine. How can we complain about being hidden when we're not doing anything to make ourselves known? How can we expect elected officials to uphold reasonable, middle-ground values when the only voices they hear are the hardliners on each side?

Acknowledging and giving voice to the Hidden Majority is not only the right thing to do, it is the only mathematically feasible solution to our broken political system. That's because the Hidden Majority is the only group in the American electorate large enough to bring about real change. No one can predict how successful such efforts might be, but if do we nothing more than introduce the concept of the Hidden Majority into the national conversation, it could have a profound impact.

So, where should we start?

PART FOUR
THE LOGISTICS

The majority of Americans are fed up with the status quo, but they have no mechanism through which to put their feelings into action.

A Hidden Majority Alliance, with its citizen-oriented agenda, could be that mechanism.

Should We Start with a New Third Party?

The Hidden Majority is a constituency in search of political representation. The natural reaction would be to form a new political party. But there are several questions we should answer before we do that:

1. America has a long-standing tradition of a two-party system, and no one is going to throw their vote away on a third party unless they believe it can win, or at least have an impact.

    How can we create a third option that will actually make a difference in our two-party system?

2. Other parties and politicians will try to co-opt our message, some with the best of intentions, some with the worst. Others will lie about our goals in an effort to undercut our movement. And political parties can be hijacked by those who want to push their own agendas, or watered down by those who lose sight of our goals.

    How can we protect our message?

3. Political movements are fertile ground for internal disagreements, competing factions, and power struggles. The faster they grow, and the bigger they get, the harder it is to stay organized and united.

    How can we keep our movement on track as it develops over time?

4. The American people do not trust the government, the parties, or the news media, nor should they. They certainly are not going to trust some new and unproven group, no matter how much they'd like to see change.

    How can we win the trust of the American people?

Before the Hidden Majority Alliance enters the political arena, it must first lay a solid foundation. It must build a true grassroots movement. It must take the time to articulate its goals and decide its policies.

In order to accomplish these things, the hub of the movement must be located outside of—and above—the political fray.

The First Step

For the reasons listed above, we believe the first step should not be a political party, but a non-political organization that can define and safeguard the principles of the Hidden Majority on an ongoing basis. This non-profit organization could serve as the hub of the movement in four vital ways:

1. **Researching Our Positions**

    As a nonpartisan think tank collecting and conducting research into the American people's true views on the issues, then articulating them as public policy positions. This information could then be used as a resource by various reform efforts, as well as by politicians, the media, and others.

2. **Rating the Players**

    As a certifying agency evaluating and publicizing how well parties, politicians, the media, and other organizations align with the desires of the Hidden Majority of Americans. This would lay bare their bias and stop parties and politicians from saying they represent the Hidden Majority when they don't.

3. **Educating the Public**

    As an educational organization informing the public on the principles and positions of the Hidden Majority and acting as the sole official voice of the movement.

4. **Networking and Coalition Building**

    As a membership organization that connects people and keeps them informed of the movement's activities and progress, as well as building a nationwide network of supporters and activists.

Such an organization could ensure that the movement stays on track as it grows, that no one hijacks its message, and that its positions are based on sound research and calm deliberation rather than political infighting.

Most importantly, such an organization could be the mechanism through which people like you can make your voices heard.

Moving Forward

The Hidden Majority Alliance could—and should—accomplish a significant portion of its agenda before it ever thinks about running political candidates:

- Introducing the concept of the Hidden Majority could give dissatisfied voters a way to express their stance in today's political landscape.

- Asking politicians and pundits how they are addressing the needs of the Hidden Majority could help temper the tone of American politics.

- Defining the views of the Hidden Majority could help people realize they belong to the movement.

- Convincing polling houses and the media to stop lumping us in with the hardliners could show the nation our true numbers.

- Building a national network could bring forth people who might be Hidden Majority candidates in the future.

If we can create a space in the public discourse for the millions of voters who desire a more balanced approach to government, the politicians will ignore us at their own risk.

After all, you don't have to win elections to affect their outcomes, and you don't have to be in office to lobby for saner policies.

Deciding Our Positions

Unlike the existing parties, a party or movement without an ideological agenda would be free to approach political and social issues in several different ways:

1) It would take a definite stance on some issues, but only when there has been a solid and long-lasting consensus among the American people. So, for example, such a party would definitely support congressional term limits.

2) It might take no stance on issues on which the people are deadlocked, or that are new and/or in flux. Its candidates could then take whatever position they like. This would allow voters to vote for the person rather than the party, something they can't really do in our current polarized system. Taking no stance would be the alliance's way of returning an issue to the marketplace of ideas.

3) It could set a range, corresponding to mainstream American values, within which its candidates and elected officials agree to operate. By guaranteeing not to go too far in either direction, we would eliminate the "slippery slope" arguments that stand in the way of commonsense reform.

It would be the responsibility of the core organization to develop the criteria for deciding when and how the Hidden Majority Alliance takes a stand. That's why it's essential that the hub of the movement remain outside the political fray.

By handling controversial issues in this way, elected officials aligned with the Hidden Majority would no longer be captive to ideological battles.

Instead, they would be free to focus on delivering basic government services effectively and efficiently.

In Conclusion: Hitting the Pause Button

- How do you stop chaos? By getting organized.

- How do you counter anger and emotion? By being rational and analytical.

- How do you replace clashing ideologies? By getting back to basics.

- How do you guide a nation that has lost its way? By pausing long enough to get your bearings.

America needs to take a break, a time-out. We need a chance to catch our collective breath, regroup, and decide together where we want to go as a nation.

This can never happen as long as every level of our government is run by parties with increasingly radical agendas. It can only happen if a new alliance, one with a non-ideological agenda, wins control of our government. It can only happen if the Hidden Majority steps forward.

It is time for us to come out of the shadows cast by the hardliners.

It is time to make ourselves known. It is time to make ourselves heard.

It is time for the Hidden Majority to stop hiding.

PART FIVE
THE FAQS

Question #1

This sounds good on paper, but is it realistic to think we can beat the major parties?

The only recommendation we've made in this document is the formation of a non-profit organization to unite and give voice to the Hidden Majority. At this point, our focus shouldn't be on the major parties at all, but on building something that truly represents the American people. What will happen from there, only time will tell.

Question #2a

Don't you know third parties can't win in America?

We're not advocating a third party at this point, but should that time ever arrive, the Hidden Majority will have an advantage over other third-party attempts.

You see, almost all third parties have been built around one person and/or one issue. They are often based on radical ideas, and even when they're not, most of them simply offer a regrouping of the usual ideological positions.

The whole point of the Hidden Majority is to take a different approach, to return to an agenda based on the desires of the American people rather than those of the organizers. As a result, a Hidden Majority party would have an advantage that neither the major parties nor the other third parties have: It would actually represent the majority of Americans.

Question #2b

But America has a two-party system—you'll never change that.

We don't want to change that. The American people don't have a problem with our two-party system; what they have a problem with is *these two parties*. There's no law saying that either or both of these parties can't be replaced when they've outlived their usefulness. The point we've made in this document is that the votes now exist to make that happen, and that those votes could, at the very least, be used to put pressure on the powers-that-be.

Question #3

Why should I trust this movement?

In today's political environment, you shouldn't trust anyone. The only thing any of us can do is watch what people and parties actually do. Luckily, the Hidden Majority approach has a built-in safeguard:

The positions of the existing parties are based on the opinions of their leaders and members, who can change them, ignore them, or lie about them at will. The positions of the Hidden Majority Alliance, on the other hand, would be based on what the American people want, as revealed by polls and other research. That means our positions will be more quantifiable, and the basis for our positions will be public knowledge.

The result will be accountability not only for politicians who claim to represent the Hidden Majority, but for the leaders of the movement itself. If they stray from these guidelines, they should be booted from the party or movement. If the party or movement does not boot them, the members of the Hidden Majority should regroup, or the American people should abandon the movement altogether.

Question #4

Haven't we had enough of poll-driven politics?

Poll-driven politics means reading the polls and telling people what they want to hear. The major parties are forced to do this because their ideological agendas don't match the values of the American people. A citizen-based party would not have to do this, because it would already be in sync with the people.

Instead of poll-driven politics, we would practice poll-driven governance, using the polls to make sure the government stays in the mainstream of American values. In our opinion, a government that doesn't utilize polls *and make changes accordingly* is not fulfilling its basic duty as a modern representative government.

But please don't misunderstand: We're not suggesting that the government should change policy every time a poll passes 50%, or that it should hold a referendum for every decision. We're not suggesting mob rule.

All we're saying is that our government should focus on the things we agree on, rather than being used as a weapon for pushing things we don't. Polls are merely one tool for making sure that happens.

Question #5

I don't trust the polls.

It is certainly true that polling houses face new challenges in a world of unlisted cell phone numbers and universal caller ID. It is also true that the Internet has facilitated the dissemination of polls from untrustworthy and incompetent sources. Worse, our politics have become so polarized that many elections are now decided within the polls' margins of error. It's hard to predict an outcome when one candidate wins the popular vote and another wins the electoral college, but it's still the pollsters who get blamed.

All of which is another reason the hub of the Hidden Majority movement must be independent of politics. We need a truly nonpartisan organization vetting the various polling groups, examining their methodology, and evaluating their accuracy. From this, the organization might identify important questions that aren't being asked, and it might even conduct its own polls.

Most importantly, when looking at poll results, the organization would break out the Hidden Majority to show that we are not just "leaners," but a distinct group with sincerely held beliefs.

Question #6

I would never vote for any candidate who does not support my strong beliefs about abortion (or gun control, etc.).

In that case, the Hidden Majority may not be for you. If you hold hardline views about one or more topics, and if your vote is determined solely by those topics, you will probably want to continue voting for the party of your choice. You might ask yourself, however, whether the current trajectory of American politics promises to resolve those issues in your favor, if at all.

Question #7

When I hear the word "majority," I worry about my civil rights. What will you do to protect the rights of minorities?

The Hidden Majority is a movement of moderates, and the polls we've quoted make it clear that these are people who believe in equal opportunity and constitutional rights. That doesn't mean they support every idea put forth, but it does mean they're not looking to dismantle existing civil rights laws. Current debates will continue, and the courts will remain the final arbiter.

Question #8

You admit that reach-across-the-aisle efforts don't work, but isn't that all this is?

Reach-across-the-aisle efforts are only necessary because the major parties no longer represent middle-ground Americans. Such efforts ask elected officials to defy the hardline values of the party that got them elected, an uncomfortable situation for all concerned. Wouldn't it be easier to have a party that already holds mainstream values?

The biggest problem with reach-across-the-aisle efforts is that they use the positions of the major parties as their starting point. Our approach is to use the positions of the American people as our starting—and ending—point.

As a result, elected officials representing the Hidden Majority wouldn't have to reach across the aisle. They would occupy the aisle and push the more radical elements of the major parties back out to the fringes, where they belong.

Question #9

What about existing reform groups, third parties, and independent politicians?

As we've said above, some of these groups and individuals have good ideas, but none of them have the voter base necessary to put pressure on the ruling powers. Only if they are part of a movement that appeals to the Hidden Majority can they truly have an impact.

Question #10

Where do you stand on election reform ideas like ranked-choice voting, open primaries, and campaign finance reform?

While the members of the Hidden Majority support election reform ideas to varying degrees, the fact is that none of these proposals really address the ideological polarization that is at the heart of our problems. And even if they did, without an authentic third option at the voting booth, these reforms could only affect the balance between the same two parties, and then only temporarily.

We believe that most election reform ideas are being pursued out of frustration. People don't see how our entrenched system can ever really be changed, so they hit around the edges. But these measures weren't in place in the past and we didn't have the degree of polarization we have today, so why would we expect them to fix it now? Hopefully in this publication we have helped clarify the core problems of our political system and pointed the way toward actually resolving them.

Question #11

Some people want to get rid of the electoral college, others want to abolish the IRS. Will a Hidden Majority Alliance have the guts to make the changes our system needs?

We believe that most of "the changes our system needs" would be unnecessary if America had a government that focused on fulfilling its responsibilities rather than pushing agendas. We question whether today's problems are a result of faults in the structure of our government, or a result of the two major parties trying to bend that structure to their advantage.

This is not to say the Hidden Majority doesn't support some of the proposed amendments and reforms. It is to say that a party representing the Hidden Majority would not come into office with grandiose promises of sweeping structural changes designed to fix all our problems. Instead, it would take each reform idea in order, look at where the voters stand on the issue, and analyze the best approach. Only when there is a well-established consensus would the government move forward.

Doesn't that sound refreshing?

Isn't it sad that it does?

Question #12

Okay, I feel like the Hidden Majority concept applies to me. What can I do to help get things started?

The first step is to share the Hidden Majority concept with the people you know. That may not seem like much, but it's actually the most important thing you can do, because nothing can happen until a significant number of people recognize themselves as being members of the Hidden Majority. Simply share the link below and get the conversation started.

For more information, visit

www.HiddenMajority.org

www.ingramcontent.com/pod-product-compliance
Lightning Source LLC
Chambersburg PA
CBHW080212040426
42333CB00043B/2617